Chiara Lubich's Communitarian Way to Holiness
in the Light of John 17:11b-19

Paloma Cabetas

Chiara Lubich's Communitarian Way to Holiness
in the Light of John 17:11b-19

NEW CITY PRESS
Hyde Park, NY

Published in the United States by New City Press
202 Comforter Blvd., Hyde Park, NY 12538
www.newcitypress.com
©2015 Paloma Cabetas

Cover design by Leandro de Leon

Library of Congress Cataloging-in-Publication Data
Cabetas, Paloma. Chiara Lubich's communitarian way to holiness--in
the light of John 17:11b-19 / by Paloma Cabetas.
     pages cm Includes bibliographical references.
   Summary: "Explores the concept expressed by Chiara Lubich that the
Lord doesn't ask us for an individual holiness, but for a communitarian
holiness in which each person must help their neighbor to become
a saint. This collective way of sanctity is explored on the thematic
elements of John 17:11b-19"-- Provided by publisher.
   ISBN 978-1-56548-581-5 (alk. paper) 1. CommunitiesxReligious
aspects--Christianity. 2. Communitarianism--Religious aspects-
-Christianity. 3. Lubich, Chiara, 1920-2008. 4. Bible. John, XVII,
11b-XIX--Criticism, interpretation, etc. 5. Holiness--Christianity. I.
Title. BV625.C28 2015 267'.182092--dc23
                                        2015014373
ISBN: 978–1–56548–581–5

Contents

Introduction

Taken from Gospel of John Chapter 17: 11b-19

Holy Father, protect them in your name that you have given me, so that they be one, as we are. [12]When I was with them, I protected them in your name that you gave me, and I guarded them, and none of them was lost if not the son of perdition, so that the scripture may be fulfilled. [13]Now I am coming to you, and I speak these things in the world, so that they may have my joy made full in them. [14]I have given them your word and the world has hated them, because they are not from the world, as I am not from the world. [15]I do not ask that you take them from the world, but that you protect them from the evil one. [16]They are not from the world as I am not from the world. [17]Sanctify them in the truth. Your word is truth. [18]As you have sent me into the world, I am sending them into the world.

[19]And for them I sanctify myself, so that they also be sanctified in truth.

> John 17:11b-19[1]

> 'Father... may they all be one' (Jn 17:11, 21). One by one those words seemed to come to life, giving us the conviction that we were born for that page of the gospel.
>
> Chiara Lubich[2]

The twentieth century brought about a revival in the Catholic world in regards to scripture. For centuries, ordinary Catholics had progressively distanced themselves from personal reading and reflection of the Bible. Exegetical studies in the time following the Reformation saw very few Catholic scholars. However, in the decades that preceded the Second Vatican Council Catholics acquired a new familiarity with scripture both in the academic realm and in their lives of piety.[3]

---

1. Unless otherwise indicated, all quotations of John's Gospel are the author's translation from *Nestle-Aland Novum Testamentum Graece,* edited by B. Aland, K. Aland, and B. Newman (Louisville, KY: American Bible Society, 2005). All other Bible quotations are taken from the New Revised Standard Version, Catholic edition.
2. Chiara Lubich, *Essential Writings* (Hyde Park, NY: New City Press, 2007), 4.
3. See for example Joseph Ratzinger, "The Transmission of Divine Revelation," in *Commentary on the*

One example of this new approach to the Bible is the Focolare Movement, founded by a young lay Italian woman, Chiara Lubich (1920–2008), in the early 1940s.

The Focolare Movement is the fruit of a living encounter with scripture and, in a particular way, with the Gospel of John. Inspired by John 17:11, 21 "May they all be one," Chiara Lubich once summarized its spirituality in the following words:

> Whenever we are asked for a definition of our spirituality, or what difference there is between the gift of God to our Movement and the gifts with which he has decorated and enriched others in the Church today and throughout the centuries, we have no hesitation in replying: unity.[4]

Chiara Lubich's spiritual proposal is not a mere reflection on scripture but a practical way of applying the gospel message to daily life. From the very beginning she invited her friends to choose a sentence of the gospel to live for a period of time and then share how they

Documents of Vatican II, ed. Herbert Vorgrimler, vol 3 (New York: Herder and Herder, 1969), 158–59.

4. Chiara Lubich, *Jesus—the Heart of His Message: Unity and Jesus Forsaken* (Hyde Park, NY: New City Press, 1997), 22.

put it into practice. This strengthened their own personal commitment but also their desire to help one another. Because of Chiara Lubich's strong call to live for unity she urged everyone, as Father Fabio Ciardi explains, "to seek out the others so that we can journey together with them towards God."[5] Such a communitarian way to holiness was quite a novelty for her time.

These pages will explore Chiara Lubich's spiritual and moral invitation to "become saints together," which stems from her reading of John 17. It will begin by analyzing the interpretation of the verb "sanctify" in that chapter of John in connection to Jesus' prayer for unity. It will then study some aspects of Chiara Lubich's spirituality and in particular her invitation to a collective way of sanctity by exploring some of the thematic elements of John 17:11b-19 as they apply to Lubich's proposal.

---

5. Fabio Ciardi, "What Kind of Holiness Comes from the Spirituality of Communion?" *Charisms in Unity* 20, no. 3 (2012): 8.

Part 1
"Sanctification"
in John 17:11b–19

Context and Structure

John 17 is called by many "the Testament of Jesus" because it concludes Jesus' farewell discourse to his disciples on the eve of his passion and death. The whole speech extends from chapter 13 to chapter 17. For the first time in John's Gospel, Jesus' words are directed only to his disciples and not to the outside world.[1]

The farewell discourse begins what exegetes traditionally call the "Book of Glory," the third and last section of the fourth gospel. Scholars refer to it as such because of the important theme of the glory of God. To express the Gospel

---

1. C.H. Dodd, *The Interpretation of the Fourth Gospel* (London: The Syndics of the Cambridge University Press, 1955), 390. The other two discourses addressed to the disciples are two brief conversations (Jacob's well in 4:31–8 and Peter's confession in 6:66–71) that, however, have more of a flavor of public revelations.

of John in one sentence, one could say that it is a progressive disclosure of the person of Jesus as the one who reveals the glory of God through his death and resurrection. The "Book of Glory" comes after the prologue and the "Book of Signs." The prologue announces the themes of the gospel, while the "signs" (σημεῖα) refer to Jesus' miracles and prepare the reader for that final hour of his glorification.

Chapter 17 contains many of the main ideas of John's Gospel. Scholars see a parallel between it and the prologue because they both summarize the theology of the whole book and announce the evangelist's way of viewing Jesus' itinerary.[2] As Ernst Käsemann points out, the theme of the glorification of Jesus—a key idea in chapter 17-takes its cue from the beginning "We beheld his glory" (1:14).[3] The difference between it and the prologue is the strong communitarian aspect of chapter 17, where Jesus is drawing his present and future disciples into his communion with the Father. As Raymond Brown states, Jesus' prayer for the disciples "is an extension of the

---

2. Thomas L. Brodie, *The Gospel According to John: A Literary and Theological Commentary* (New York: Oxford University Press, 1997), 508.

3. Ernst Käsemann, *The Testament of Jesus: A Study of the Gospel of John in the Light of Chapter 17* (Philadelphia: Fortress Press, 1968), 6.

prayer for his own glorification."[4] In fact, Jesus will be glorified on earth through the disciples' mission, as Jesus himself affirms: "I have been glorified in them" (17:10).

Another thematic element that shows the progression towards a more communitarian view can be seen in the relationship between faith and love. Although the fourth gospel focuses on faith, the latter half of the gospel seems to move the emphasis from faith to love. In fact, the verb πιστεύω ("to believe") or related adjective πιστός ("faithful, believer") appears 76 times in the first part of the gospel (chapters 1 through 12) versus 24 times in the second part, while ἀγαπάω ("to love") or the noun ἀγάπη ("love") occur 6 times only in the first half and 35 times in the second.[5]

Important in this sense is the vine/branches image in chapter 15, which precedes and pre-

---

4. Raymond E. Brown, "The Gospel According to John XIII-XXI," *Anchor Bible Series,* vol 29A (Garden City: Anchor Bible, 1966), 763.

5. The author's count is slightly different from the exegete Gérard Rossé, who counts only the appearance of the verbs. See Gérard Rossé, *The Spirituality of Communion: a New Approach to the Johannine Writings* (Hyde Park, NY: New City Press, 1998), 64. The contrast is also evident when, besides ἀγαπάω we include the similar verb φιλέω ("to love") which appears 4 times in the first half and 8 times in the second.

pares the reader for the prayer in chapter 17.
Faith is necessary but it is true faith when it
brings the believer to love: love for Jesus and
mutual love. Pope Benedict XVI sees 15:9 ("As
the Father has loved me, so I have loved you;
abide in my love") as the point of connection
of the parable of the vine with Jesus' prayer for
unity. According to his view, an explanation of
"abiding in Jesus' love" can be seen in John 17:26:
"I made your name known to them, and I will
make it known, so that the love with which you
have loved me may be in them, and I in them."
Therefore the vine discourse is aiming at the
unity emphasized in chapter 17.[6]

Although inserted in the final address of Jesus
to his disciples, chapter 17 stands out from the
rest of that discourse. Thomas L. Brodie notes
that the previous chapters are paired, forming
diptychs (13 matches 14; 15:1—16:4a matches
16:4b—33), while 17 does not have an equivalent.
The other chapters contain dialogue, while chapter 17 is in the form of a long, continuous prayer,
the only one in John's Gospel. The beginning
of the chapter marks this clearly, noting that
Jesus "looked up to heaven" (17:1). Brodie sees
an upward movement towards heaven, beginning with the lifting of the eyes, progressing

---

6. Ratzinger, Joseph (Pope Benedict XVI), *Jesus of Nazareth*, (New York: Doubleday, 2007), 263.

with a sense of Jesus' coming to the Father, and concluding with expressions of sovereignty and equality with the Father, as if Jesus is already sitting at his right hand.[7]

These brief pages cannot address the multiple and complex thematic elements of chapter 17; therefore they will be limited to analyzing the theme of "sanctification" as it appears in verses 11b-19, with the intent to show the intrinsic connection of sanctification with the theme of unity which is so prominent in this chapter of John.

Meaning of "Sanctification" in John 17:11b-19

Chapter 17 may be divided into three parts: Jesus prays for himself (1–5), for his disciples (6–19) and for those who will come to believe in him (20–26).

The first mention of sanctity in chapter 17 is in verse 11b, when Jesus addresses the Father as ἅγιε ("Holy"). Ratzinger, in fact, explains that in the Bible holiness is an attribute of God alone. Sanctifying is the action of handing over persons or objects to God, setting them aside from the ordinary everyday aspects of life.[8]

---

7. Brodie, *Gospel According to John,* 506.
8. Ratzinger, Joseph (Pope Benedict XVI), *Jesus of Nazareth. Part Two: Holy Week—from the Entrance into Jerusalem to the Resurrection* (San Francisco: Ignatius Press, 2011), 86.

The verb ἁγιάζω ("sanctify") appears three times in the middle part of chapter 17, when Jesus is praying for his disciples. Translations vary: "sanctify," "consecrate" or "make holy." All these convey the same concept: bringing something ordinary into God's realm.

John's Gospel contains only one other appearance of ἁγιάζω outside of this chapter in 10:36: "the one whom the Father has sanctified and sent into the world." Here, the subject is the Father and the object of sanctification is the Son.

In the first mention of ἁγιάζω in verse 17 ("Sanctify them in the truth"), the Father acts as the subject and the disciples act as the object of the sanctification action. Verse 19 introduces a new element: "For their sakes I sanctify myself." The subject is now Jesus himself and he is also the object of the action. This is followed by the passive use of the verb (ἡγιασμένοι), where the sanctification action is directed to the disciples: "so that they may also be sanctified in truth."

The very unusual form of ἁγιάζω at the beginning of verse 19, followed by the reflexive pronoun (ἐμαυτόν) and with Jesus as the subject, is found only once in John's writings and very rarely in other New Testament texts.

There are divergent interpretations of its meaning in this case, already dating back to the patristic era. John Chrysostom explains it like this: "He means, 'I offer to you a sacrifice.'… In

[Old Testament times], sanctification was typo-
logically indicated by the sheep. But now it is
not in type but in truth itself."[9] For Chrysostom,
the context suggests this interpretation, because
these verses precede the passion narrative: "It
is clear from what follows that he was alluding
to his own sacrifice when he said, 'I sanctify'."[10]

However, not all the patristic commentaries
make the connection with the Old Testament
sacrifices. Ambrose, for example, establishes
a distinction between the divine and human
nature in Jesus; it is, according to Ambrose, "not
the Godhead but the flesh that needed sanctification" although, "by virtue of his divinity,"[11]
Jesus also has the power to sanctify his disciples.
Cyril of Alexandria and Augustine concentrate
on Jesus' unity with his disciples. Cyril sees it
as the disciples receiving Jesus' gift:

> Christ called down on us the ancient
> gift of humanity, that is, sanctification
> through the Spirit and communion with
> the divine nature, his disciples being

---

9. John Chrysostom, Homily 82 on the Gospel of John.
Quoted in Joel C. Elowsky, ed., *John 11–21*, vol. 4b of
Ancient Christian Commentary on Scripture (Down-
ers Grove, IL: InterVarsity Press, 2007), 253.

10. Ibid.

11. Saint Ambrose, *Exposition of the Christian Faith*,
Book II, chapter 9, §72, in *Ancient Christian Commentary*, 254.

the first to receive it… he is seen as the beginning and the gate and the way of every good thing for us—he is inspired to add what follows, namely, the words "for their sake I consecrate myself."[12]

For Augustine, Jesus' sanctity extends to the disciples as members of his body, the Church. He adds, explaining it with a rhetorical question that affirms this:

What does he mean by the words "and for their sake I sanctify myself" but I sanctify them in myself, since they are also myself?[13]

Most modern commentators, beginning with Bultmann, take for granted John Chrysostom's reading. Bultmann explains that ἁγιάζω together with ὑπὲρ αὐτῶν ("for their sake") means "making holy" in the sense of "consecrating for the sacrifice."[14] Many others follow this interpreta-

---

12. Cyril of Alexandria, *Commentary on the Gospel of Saint John,* Book XI, chapter 10, in *Ancient Christian Commentary,* 253–54.
13. Saint Augustine, *Tractate 108 on the Gospel of John,* no. 5, in *Ancient Christian Commentary,* 254.
14. Rudolf Bultmann, *The Gospel of John: a Commentary* (Philadelphia: Westminster John Knox Press, 1971), 510, note 5.

tion.[15] C.K. Barrett indicates that most Jewish precedents which contain the expression "sanctify" followed by the reflexive pronoun generally have an ethical sense, but in the end Barrett agrees with the sacrificial interpretation because of the immediate circumstances following the discourse.

It seems most plausible that Jesus is speaking of himself as a victim preparing for the sacrifice.[16] This idea is repeated in Hebrews 10:10, "We have been sanctified through the offering of the body of Jesus Christ once for all."

Another interpretation of the word ἁγιάζω is however acquiring ever more relevance among contemporary exegetes. According to them, the identification of the word with the Old Testament rites neglects the context and the continuity with verse 17.[17]

---

15. Thus, Rudolf Schnackenburg, *The Gospel According to St. John: Volume 3* (New York: Crossroad/Herder & Herder, 1983), 187; Ratzinger, *Jesus of Nazareth Part Two*, 87–88; Brown, "Gospel According to John," 767.

16. C.K. Barrett, *The Gospel According to St John* (London: SPCK Publishing, 1988), 511.

17. See, for example, Gail R. O' Day, "The Gospel of John: Introduction, Commentary and Reflections," in *The New Interpreter's Bible: A Commentary in Twelve Volumes*, vol. 9 (Nashville, Tennessee: Abingdon Press, 2001), 794; Ignace de la Potterie, *La Vérité dans Saint Jean* (Rome: Biblical Institute Press, 1977), 761–62; Rossé, *Spirituality of Communion*, 84; Harold W. Attridge, "How Priestly Is the 'High Priestly Prayer'

Reviewing the context in which ἀγιάζω ἐμαυτόν is placed, I agree with these later commentaries that reading ἀγιάζω with the sense of a ritual sacrifice is stretching the meaning of the word and taking it out of its immediate context. The verb ἀγιάζω appears three consecutive times, very close to one another. The first and third time (verse 17 and verse 19b), ἀγιάζω refers to the disciples, while only the second time—verse 19a, in the reflexive form and referred to Jesus—do scholars identify it with cultic animal sacrifices. The term is also closely linked to "truth," with which it appears associated in the first and third mention of the word, as we will read below.

Obviously, the sense of the sacrifice of Christ cannot be totally ignored, either. The words ὑπὲρ αὐτῶν ("for their sake") and the location of the farewell discourse immediately preceding the passion are facts that strongly affirm this identification. John's Gospel is all oriented to the "hour" in which Christ showed his love for humanity in a supreme way. The passion and death are his sacrifice and he is undoubtedly referring to this moment when he indicates he is sanctifying himself. Therefore, the suffering and sacrifice of Christ on the cross for the sake

of John 17?" *The Catholic Biblical Quarterly* 75, no. 1 (2013): 14.

of his disciples (those present and those who will come throughout history) is part of the meaning.

What I reject however is the identification of Christ's holiness with an old rite that Jesus' life and actions have overcome. Through the farewell discourse, Jesus is giving us a deeper truth. Without entering into the lengthy debate about the priestly character of chapter 17, one could affirm with Harold Attridge that, although Christ's disciples share in his priesthood, "what makes them so is not any ritual function but their participation in the truth that Christ reveals... It makes them one and makes them holy." [18]

The unusual form of ἁγιάζω would therefore indicate the divine unity between Father and Son, which then extends to the disciples. Although commentaries throughout history tended to focus on Christ's sanctification as a personal sacrifice, this contemporary reading seems to reflect what Cyril of Alexandria and Augustine had already noted: the strong communitarian emphasis of ἁγιάζω.

---

18. Attridge, "High Priestly Prayer," 14.

Themes Connected with "Sanctification" in John 17:11b-19

Sanctification and Unity

Holiness does not, therefore, separate the individual from the rest of the community. The first appearance of the word "Holy" referring to the Father in verse 11 is connected to the request "protect them in your name… that they be one." Besides, as it was mentioned above, in verse 19 the explicit reference to Jesus' sanctity includes the disciples: "for them I sanctify myself, so that they may also be sanctified (...)." These two factors lead Brodie to conclude that "the process of making holy, far from leading to isolation, is closely linked to unity."[19]

From the beginning of chapter 17, Jesus is no longer addressing his disciples as in the preceding chapters, but he speaks directly to the Father. Dodd points out the similarities with Hellenistic forms such as the Hermetic writings, in which a dialogue usually concludes with a prayer or hymn. The difference in this case is that the dialogue is not a private conversation between two individuals, but this whole discourse has a clear corporate character.[20]

---

19. Brodie, *Gospel According to John*, 431.
20. Dodd, *Fourth Gospel*, 421–22.

The communitarian aspect of this passage, as well as the marked contrast of Jesus' disciples with "the world," has generated various interpretations as to the nature of the community for which John was writing. Some commentators, including Rudolf Bultmann, found a Gnostic influence in John's writings.[21] Bultmann in fact points us to texts from the Mandaean literature—produced by one of the Gnostic groups—which contain the same idea of love for an elect group of friends.[22] Later studies, however, lead to very different conclusions. Brown, for example, analyzing the early Christian groups, explains that unity, referring to the community, is not an idea which was exclusive to Gnosticism. A comparison with the Qumran documents shows this. Until the discovery of the Dead Sea Scrolls after World War II, John's accent on "being one"—a concept which was not emphasized in the Old Testament—seemed to be the influence of Greek philosophers like Pythagoras and the Stoics, and of Gnosticism. However, in the Qumran texts, there is a Jewish source that is somehow contemporary to John's Gospel (both texts are dated around the first centuries of the Christian era) and where the term *yaḥad* ("unity") appears

21. In the first centuries of Christianity, Gnostics formed groups who believed an exclusive knowledge gave them the key to salvation.
22. Bultmann, *Gospel of John*, 487.

frequently. There are many interpretations of this word as it shows on the Qumran scrolls, but the general impression is that it refers to a community of men united by the same lifestyle and observance of the Law.[23]

To explain John's emphasis on "being one," Raymond Brown also says that the gospel was addressed mostly to people who already believed in Jesus in order to help them deepen their faith and see the contrast with their previous beliefs.[24]

Sanctification in Truth

The importance of unity of belief can be seen in the fact that, in both verses 17 and 19, ἁγιάζω is linked to ἀλήθεια ("truth"). In verse 17, Jesus asks the Father to sanctify them "in the truth" which is equal to God's word. As noted by Brown, the identification of the truth with God's word also finds a parallel in the Jewish tradition as a Jewish prayer for the new year: "Purify our hearts to serve you in truth. You, O God, are truth [Jer 10:10], and your word is truth and stands forever."[25]

---

23. For a detailed analysis of the use of the word "one" see the sources quoted by Brown, "Gospel According to John," 777.
24. Raymond E. Brown, *An Introduction to the Gospel of John*, ed. Francis Moloney (New York: Anchor Bible, 2003), 182.
25. Brown, "Gospel According to John," 765.

God is not sanctifying the disciples by any visible ceremony but by their acceptance of the truth. This, Schnackenburg points out, has some similarities with the Gnostic communities, but also a great difference. The evangelist is not referring to some mysterious, esoteric knowledge; he identifies the truth with God's word ("your word is truth" 17:17). In the context of John's Gospel, the truth is the person of the Son, as affirmed in 14:6 ("I am the Truth") and in the prologue's identification of God's word with Jesus. One could therefore assert with Schnackenburg that, in John's Gospel, the person of Jesus replaces the sanctifying effect of the Torah.[26]

De la Potterie, in his study of "truth" in John's writings, affirms that John's reflection on truth is the opposite of an abstract speculation; for John, truth is an earthly reality. It has to do with the revelation of Jesus to humankind for our salvation. Truth needs an interiorization process, but this does not mean a withdrawal into the spiritual world. For de la Potterie, truth in John is the revelation of love. When a person welcomes truth, he or she is welcoming a seed that will produce the fruit of mutual love.[27] We

---

26. Schnackenburg, *Gospel According to John,* 185.
27. De la Potterie, *La Vérité,* 1014.

therefore see here yet another connection to a communitarian lifestyle.

Sanctification in the World

One other theme closely linked to consecration is the distinction between the disciples and "the world." In the action of sanctifying or handing over a person or object to God there is already an implicit separation from the world. John makes it explicit throughout his entire gospel, and in a very clear way in chapter 17, where Jesus refuses to pray for the world (17:9) and asks the Father to protect his disciples from the evil one (17:15), repeating that they do not belong to the world (17:14, 16) . At the same time, there is a clear sense of mission to the world in 17:18, "As you have sent me into the world, I am sending them into the world", and the unity Jesus prays for is so that "the world may believe" (17:21). Are these two approaches contradictory?

Regarding the separation from the world, many commentators note the danger of a dualism that John's negative attitude toward the world can create. As mentioned above, Bultmann, among others, thinks that the Johannine's community was a Gnostic community. Käsemann holds the same opinion—as Schnackenburg reports—of the Johannine community as an "inward-turning, esoteric group that was withdrawn from the world of unbelievers … in other words, a 'Christian mystery-community'."[28] Brown, who rejects this interpretation, claims nonetheless that a group of Johannine disciples separated from the community. Brown bases his opinion on his reading of John's letters, which seem to reproach the secessionist group for their lack of love for their brethren. The members of the group, in his opinion, justified their views by basing them on John's Gospel.[29]

In explaining the reasons for such a secession, Brown notes that, contrary to what happens in the Synoptics, there is a lack of stress on ethical behavior in John's Gospel. The ethical emphasis for John is on mutual love, which for him was the main commandment on which all others depended. In the Johannine writings, Brown states, the love commandment refers to those in the community and not to the others. There is not a command to love one's enemies as in Matthew 5:44, not even to love our neighbor as in Matthew 19:19. Moreover, John 17:9 tells of Jesus' refusal to pray for the world.[30]

---

28. Ernst Käsemann, *Jesu letzter Wille nach Johannes 17* (Tubingen: JCB Mohr, 1966), 119, quoted in Schnackenburg, *Gospel According to John*, 213.

29. Raymond E. Brown, *The Community of the Beloved Disciple* (New York: Paulist Press, 1979), 106.

30. Ibid., 133.

Gérard Rossé comes to the defense of the evangelist. He claims that the omission of the other commandments does not mean the community wants to separate itself as a sectarian group, but derives from the fact that John's Gospel focuses mainly on the life of the followers of Christ. According to Rossé, Jesus is not asking the disciples to withdraw from the world; he is giving them a mission to the world. It is not a mission of proclamation but of revealing the good news. Believers are "in a state of mission by reason of their being one."[31]

Therefore, although in John there is a marked contrast between those who accept Jesus' message and those who do not, there is also a more universal view of the outside world in John's writings. There are many passages that attest to it, besides the parts of chapter 17 quoted above. We see it clearly in 20:21 ("As the Father has sent me, so I send you") but also in 4:38 ("I sent you to reap that for which you did not work") and in 15:20 ("If they persecuted me, they will persecute you, too; if they fulfilled my word, they will fulfill yours, too"). In Jesus' discourse to Nicodemus, we see not only the sense of mission, but God's love for the world (in 3:16 "God so loved the world that he gave his only Son," and in verse 17 he adds that his goal was not

---

31. Rossé, *Spirituality of Communion*, 87.

"to condemn the world," but "that the world might be saved through him.") This sense of mission, I believe, is the key to reconciling the particularism of an election of a few with the universal approach that Christ's call is directed to all humanity.

The concept of mission is closely linked to the idea of sanctification. For example, the "mission sentence" of chapter 17 ("As you have sent me into the world, I am sending them into the world", 17:18) is the verse between the two mentions of ἁγιάζω. Ratzinger offers an explanation of this, affirming that God's sanctifying action "also includes the essential dynamic of 'existing for'."[32]

De la Potterie also notes the parallel with 10:36 ("the one whom the Father has sanctified and sent into the world") where there is the only other mention of the word "sanctification" in John's Gospel. Also there, it refers to Jesus and is connected to his mission.[33] Unlike in chapter 10, however, where the term is applied only to the Son, chapter 17 mentions "sanctification" of both Jesus and the community of the disciples. D.A. Carson explains the difference between the two:

---

32. Ratzinger, *Jesus of Nazareth Part Two,* 86.
33. De la Potterie, *La Vérité,* 763.

> Jesus' own sanctification is not a step which makes him holier, but rather one which establishes the basis for his disciples' sanctification… and their sanctification has as its goal, witness to the world.[34]

Therefore, while aware of the dangers that a narrow reading of John's Gospel can provoke, we can agree that John portrays a missionary outreach. It is precisely because of the unity of the believers that the disciples, participating in Jesus' glory, can be witnesses of God's love to the world. Important in this regard—we can affirm with O'Grady—is that in order for this mission to happen mutual love is essential.[35] As Brown says, Jesus was a challenge to the world; now that Jesus makes his disciples partakers of his unity with the Father, the challenge to the world is the Christian community as such.[36]

---

34. D.A. Carson, *The Farewell Discourse and Final Prayer of Jesus: an Exposition of John 14–17* (Grand Rapids, Mich.: Baker Book House, 1980), 193.
35. John F. O'Grady, "Individual and Community in John" (Ph.D. diss., Pontifical Biblical Institute, Rome, 1978), 71.
36. Brown, "Gospel According to John," 778.

Summary

From this analysis we can see that there is a planned progression in John's vision. It was stated above that chapter 17 mirrors the prologue. The difference, as many note, is that while the prologue places the emphasis on the beginning of history (before the Incarnation), here there is the fulfillment of the final unity. This unity now encompasses the portion of humanity redeemed by Jesus. The story of salvation that the prologue narrates in chapter 17 is applied to the whole community, and unity is the visible sign of this sanctification. It is the sign of God's life.

The concept of "sanctification" is therefore a necessary step to include humanity in the life that, before the Incarnation, was reserved to the relationship between the divine persons. John is deliberately and progressively bringing that portion of the world that has welcomed Christ's message into the realm of the divine. This is manifested in their sanctification in unity.

Part 2
Chiara Lubich's "Holy Journey" in the Light of John 17:11b–19

Sanctity and unity, two themes that John's Gospel highlights, are essential elements in the spirituality that Chiara Lubich proposes. From its very beginning, this spiritual way was strongly influenced by her reading of John's Gospel and in particular of chapter 17. The sections that follow attempt a summary of the main ways in which Lubich understood and connected these two themes in her life and teachings.

A Brief History

Chiara (as people like to call her familiarly) began her spiritual journey during the Second World War. In the heavily bombarded city of Trent, in northern Italy, Chiara and her friends faced the possibility of death at any moment. Amongst the ruin and devastation that surrounded them, they rediscovered the revelation of God as Love and felt called to make him the ideal of their young lives. Whenever they had to rush to the air-raid shelters, together they opened the small book of the gospels and read the divine words they contained. The gospel sentences that refer to love—love of neighbor and Jesus' new commandment of mutual love—stood out in a particular way for them.[1]

It is very significant that Chiara's spiritual way focused on the gospel, more than on the manuals of spirituality that were more common at the time. This provoked criticism from the people around her group of friends, and even resulted in complaints to the Church authorities. Chiara explains that, while their emphasis on unity and their sharing of goods provoked the accusation that they were communists, their fervor in reading the gospel and putting its words into practice made traditional Catholics consider them Protestants.[2]

One day in a dark cellar by candle light they read the prayer of Jesus before he died. "Father... may they all be one" (Jn 17:11, 21). Those words, so difficult to understand for people not versed in exegetical studies, seemed addressed to them. Chiara saw in them Jesus' "final testament, the most precious desire of God who gave his life for

---

1. Lubich, *Essential Writings*, 5.
2. Ibid., 351.

us."[3] She was conscious that it was a divine plan, which went beyond their human strength. A few days later, on the feast of Christ the King, Chiara and her friends, as they gathered around the altar, offered God their lives so that he could use them to build unity. Describing that moment, Chiara would later attest:

> One thing was clear in our hearts: what God wanted for us was unity. We live for the sole aim of being one with him, one with each other, and one with everyone. This marvelous vocation linked us to heaven and immersed us in the one human family. What purpose in life could be greater? As far as we are concerned, no ideal is more than this.[4]

The thrust to live unity was decisive for the small Christian community that was forming around her. In Chiara's early letters, the cry "Unity or death!" often appeared.[5] She felt the strong desire to emulate the first Christians, recalling how they "are not remembered so much for going into ecstasy but for how much

---

3. Ibid., 99.
4. Ibid., 17.
5. See, for example, Chiara Lubich, *Early Letters: at the Origins of a New Spirituality* (Hyde Park, NY: New City Press, 2012), 59, 75, 90.

they loved one another: they had grasped, in its first freshness, the testament of Jesus."[6]

A Sanctity that is "Collective"

Very early on, as the testament of Jesus helped Chiara understand the spiritual road that God had prepared for her, she and her friends began to instinctively refuse the way of sanctity that had traditionally been taught to them. They were afraid that they would tend to look at themselves and their own perfection instead of being rooted in love. In a 1948 letter to a Franciscan priest, with surprising authority for a young lay woman, Chiara admonished,

> Don't try to determine by yourself whether or not you're going forward. It's subtle pride. … Never desire perfection. Desire to love Him.[7]

Her fear was that a thrust to sanctity would bring people to isolate themselves from others. If God wanted Chiara to aim at sanctity, she said, it would have to be as a consequence of love of neighbor. She realized that God was showing to her a collective spiritual way.[8]

---

6. Lubich, *Essential Writings*, 87.
7. Lubich, *Early Letters*, 126.
8. Chiara Lubich, *Santi Insieme* (Rome: Città Nuova Editrice, 1994), 75.

A collective sanctity, for Chiara, meant sanctity "out of love,"[9] where a person's individual effort served as an example and a help to his or her contemporaries and also to those who would come in the future. It implied, Chiara explained, becoming saints not for self-pleasure but for the glory of God and for the good of our brothers and sisters.[10]

At the same time, she understood sanctity as "the purpose of a Christian life on earth."[11] Sanctity for her was not reserved for great figures of the past, but it was a call for every Christian to live the love Jesus preached, as this writing from the 1950s affirms:

> In God's eyes "human being," "Christian" and "saint" are synonyms. "Holiness! It's just a word…" say many, very many people. No. Christ does not ask us the impossible! Furthermore, we must rid ourselves of a certain idea of holiness inherited from the past. Phenomena such as miracles, ecstasies, visions do not constitute holiness. Holiness lies in perfect love.[12]

---

9. Ibid., 76.
10. Ibid.
11. Lubich, *Essential Writings*, 71.
12. Ibid., 272–73.

Many years later, at the end of 1980 and once the foundations of the Movement were firmly established, Chiara asked God to help her by giving her "a decisive push towards holiness."[13] In her typical, communitarian way, she soon invited all the Focolare members, scattered throughout the world, to be part of this "Holy Journey"[14] through a monthly conference call, where she disclosed her insights and profound experiences of her own itinerary towards God. She invited all, young and old, to join her in living those strong spiritual promptings.

In one of these conference calls, in 1998, she confided her initial rejection of seeking "sanctity for the sake of sanctity."[15] It was also clear for her that "sanctity as a fact depends more on God than on us. So we should never cease asking him for it as his gift."[16] The way par excellence in aiming at sanctity was love. Chiara explained:

13. Lucia Abignente, "Journeying Towards Holiness Together: Chiara Lubich's Witness," *Charisms in Unity* 20, no. 3 (2012): 19.
14. She called it "Holy Journey" inspired by Psalm 84:5, "Blessed those who find their strength in you, whose hearts are set on pilgrimage" (New Jerusalem Bible; the Italian translation Lubich used read "Holy Journey.") See Chiara Lubich, *Journey: Spiritual Insights* (New York: New City Press, 1984), 19.
15. Chiara Lubich, "Holiness of the Masses," *Charisms in Unity* 20, no. 3 (2012): 22.
16. Chiara Lubich, *Journey to Heaven: Spiritual Thoughts to Live* (Hyde Park, NY: New City Pr., 1997), 94.

Conscious of the fact that ours is a communitarian way and one that requires us to live to perfection the command to love our neighbor as ourselves, it became clear to me that in order to become a saint I would have to desire this same goal for my neighbors as I do for myself.[17]

Johannine Themes in Chiara Lubich's Concept of Sanctity

Sanctification and Unity

For Chiara, therefore, sanctity—an ardent desire for a fervent young woman—became soon identified with unity, as she wrote already in April 1948:

Enjoy your unity, but for God and not for yourselves... Our unity too, which is our sanctity, should be loved for God! Let's make the Unity between us (which gives us the fullness of joy, peace, and strength) the springboard to run and jump to wherever there is not unity, and make it happen there![18]

---

17. Lubich, "Holiness of the Masses," 22.
18. Lubich, *Early Letters*, 98.

This was unheard of in those days. In the Italian pre-conciliar Church where Chiara was raised, the word "unity" had almost disappeared from the vocabulary. As Marco Tecilla—also from Trent and the first young man to follow in Chiara's footsteps—would explain many years later, in their "traditional Christian environment, talking about sanctity meant talking about penance, continuous prayer, miracles, about a life withdrawn from the world."[19]

A study of the history of moral theology by the Dominican Servais Pinckaers offers an understanding of this phenomenon in Christianity. Pinckaers maintained that the late Middle Ages provoked a profound change in the conception of ethics, a change that would have longstanding consequences until the present day. That change was partly the result of the fragmentation of Saint Thomas of Aquinas' work, no longer studied as an organic unity, and especially of William of Ockham's nominalism, which had a deep influence on all subsequent moral systems. Nominalism shifted the emphasis from the objective goal at which human beings aim to the subjective intention of the individual. This subjectivism also indirectly challenged a morality of happiness and the centrality of

---

19. Marco Tecilla, "Santificarsi Insieme: Alcuni Strumenti," *Gen's* 34, no. 3/4 (2004): 68.

love. Morality became based on the obligation imposed by God's will and not on the pursuit of happiness.[20]

Although moral theologians, past and present, generally agree in giving love the primary role, in reality, Pinckaers affirms, this does not happen. The morality of obligation that was prevalent for many centuries too often associated love with sex and therefore avoided promoting the emphasis on love. It became more preoccupied with defining and avoiding sin than with explaining virtue and leading people to their ultimate end. Love was mistrusted and no longer needed to attain salvation.[21] A significant example is this quote from the fifteenth century devotional book, *The Imitation of Christ*:

> One holy man said: 'Each time I have been in the company of people, I have come away less of a person myself...' Therefore, our Lord and his angels will draw near and abide with those who withdraw from their acquaintances and their friends.[22]

20. Servais Pinckaers, *The Sources of Christian Ethics* (Washington, DC: Catholic University of America Press, 1995), 415.
21. Ibid., 29.
22. *The Imitation of Christ* I, XX, 1–6, quoted in Chiara Lubich, *A New Way: the Spirituality of Unity* (Hyde Park, NY: New City Press, 2006), 25–26.

This moral approach was also highly individualistic. Looking at the history of spirituality, Thomas Norris states that

> ...the spiritual journey was an individual one. True, the community could help, indeed, had to help. But in the final analysis ... Catholicism, the most social of all religions, had in fact become an individual "way."[23]

Chiara's identification of sanctity with unity is then quite new in the history of spiritualities, but is very much in keeping with the Johannine spirit. As our analysis of chapter 17 shows, John's Gospel closely links the theme of holiness with the theme of unity. With this approach, sanctification becomes the opposite of a process conducive to isolating individuals.

The definition of "unity" in John's writings plays an important role. For the evangelist, as Käsemann points out, unity is much more than friendship or even a covenant. He affirms that it has the "quality and mark of the heavenly reality," adding that "if unity exists on earth, then it can only exist as a projection from heaven,

---

23. Thomas J. Norris, *The Trinity—Life of God, Hope for Humanity: Towards a Theology of Communion* (Hyde Park, NY: New City Press, 2009), 57.

that is, as the mark and object of revelation."[24] Ratzinger offers this explanation:

> Unity can only come from the Father through the Son. It has to do with the "glory" that the Son gives: with his presence, granted through the Holy Spirit, which is the fruit of the Cross, the fruit of Jesus' transformation through death and Resurrection.[25]

Dodd states that "the archetypal relation between Father and Son which is everywhere affirmed in the Book of Signs… is now declared to be realized in the disciples."[26]

From the beginning of her experience, Chiara followed John's Gospel closely, explaining that unity is a reflection of the relations that exist among the persons of the Holy Trinity. "Jesus really brought the 'law of Heaven' to earth," she wrote. "It is the life of the Most Holy Trinity that we must try to imitate by loving one another, with the grace of God, as the Persons of the Most Holy Trinity love one another."[27]

For Chiara, it was clear that unity was a gift from God, not brought about by any human

---

24. Käsemann, *The Testament of Jesus,* 68.
25. Ratzinger, *Jesus of Nazareth Part Two*, 95–96.
26. Dodd, *Gospel According to John,* 397.
27. Lubich, *A New Way*, 50.

effort. She often exhorted her followers to live in such a way that "Christ may continue through us the work of creating unity in this world."[28] She also saw a difference between the ethical commandment to live mutual love and unity as a gift from God:

> When we live the new commandment, striving to welcome the Father's gift of unity in Jesus, the life of the Trinity is no longer lived only in the inner life of the individual but flows freely among the members of the Mystical Body of Christ.[29]

Gérard Rossé's analysis of the farewell discourse offers a similar view. According to Rossé, John makes a clear and careful distinction between reciprocal love and unity. The first part of the farewell discourse, continuing to chapter 17, has Jesus commanding his disciples to live mutual love. This is a mandate on his part. Unity, instead, is not something that he can ask of his disciples, but a gift he prays to obtain from God. Unity goes beyond ethics, even if it is intrinsically connected to ethics, because unity cannot happen without mutual love.[30]

---

28. Lubich, *Essential Writings,* 63.
29. Ibid., 205.
30. Rossé, *Spirituality of Communion,* 79–80.

Sanctification in Truth

Chiara's emphasis on love does not detract from the truth. On the contrary, already in one of her first letters, she affirmed:

> Let's act: Let our love be truth and let it be deeds! *"Little children, let us love, not in word or speech, but in truth and action"* (1 Jn 3:18). Why are we afraid to say to everyone that we are only passing through here below and that there above we will be staying forever? Why not enlighten our brothers' blindness, if we have the Light and if we are the Light?[31]

The identification of love with deeds and with truth shows the influence of John's writings; Chiara, in fact, is quoting the First Epistle of John. The sanctification Jesus asks for his disciples in chapter 17 is a sanctification "in the truth," as the evangelist repeats twice (in verse 17 and in verse 19).

John's concept of truth, which becomes identified with God's words to humanity, is very important to balance a contemporary view of love that can easily fall into sentimentalism.

---

31. Lubich, *Early Letters*, 12.

Pinckaers explains that, as a reaction to the mistrust placed on love and passions in the past, contemporary Christian ethicists have often fallen into the opposite extreme. They have tried to avoid the excessive preoccupation with sin that a morality of obligation alone imposes and they focus on love as the center of Christianity. However, some arrive at considering love as an emotion which excludes a person from the obligations that the commandments—and natural law itself—impose on human beings. Such excess of subjectivism leads to denying the beauty of the law in perfecting human love.[32]

Chiara Lubich spoke of love continuously but insisted that Christian love is not just a feeling or emotion, but it is "synonymous with sacrifice"[33] because it imitates the love of the crucified Christ. This view was present from the very beginning. One of her first letters reads:

> In this way, and only in this way, doing the truth, we are able to love. Otherwise love is just empty sentimentalism. Whereas real Love is Christ Jesus, it's the Truth, it's the gospel![34]

---

32. Pinckaers, *Christian Ethics,* 29.
33. Chiara Lubich, *On the Holy Journey* (New York: New City Press, 1988), 157.
34. Lubich, *Early Letters,* 120.

Chiara, in fact, invited the members of the Focolare Movement to practice what she called the "moment of truth," a way of fraternal correction. Imitating the example of the early Christians, she suggested they tell one another, moved only by their mutual love, what is positive and what is not so positive in them, in order to help one another progress in sanctity. Emphasizing, as always, the communitarian aspect of this spirituality, she quoted an African proverb, "Our brother is like an eye in the back of our head," explaining that the other members of the community can often help us see and understand what we cannot see for ourselves.[35]

Sanctification in the World

Living the truth has as a consequence a certain separation from the negative aspects of the world. This separation, noted above as part of John's concept of holiness, is also explicit in Chiara's writings. In an address to Focolare members in 1983, she encouraged those who were new to pursuing a life of holiness to protect their spiritual lives by "keeping far away from us the things or persons that were a cause of temptation in our past life: unhealthy friendships, various little vices," etc. and to instead

---

35. Thomas Masters and Amy Uelmen, *Focolare: Living a Spirituality of Unity in the United States* (Hyde Park, NY: New City Press, 2011), 48.

nourish it "with our unity with those who share our spirituality."[36]

Unity among those who tend to holiness is, therefore, necessary for Chiara. However, a narrow interpretation of this unity could bring about that same danger of sectarianism that historians point out may have existed among the first Christians as a consequence of some readings of John's Gospel. Misinterpreted mutual love and separation from other lifestyles can lead people who want to "become saints together" to forming groups that are closed in on themselves and feel superior to others. In fact, in a study of the Focolare and other ecclesial movements born in the twentieth century, Brendan Leahy states that they have been accused of being the kind of sects that isolate their members from the world.[37]

One could argue, first of all, that the unity of such movements with the Magisterium of the Church and the Church's approval shows that they are not sects. In addition, a reading of Chiara's writings and the fruits of the Focolare Movement founded by her—where a 360° dialogue is active throughout the world—shows that more often than not the result of practicing

---

36. Lubich, *Journey*, 86.
37. Brendan Leahy, *Ecclesial Movements and Communities: Origins, Significance and Issues* (Hyde Park, NY: New City Press, 2011), 129.

what she taught is the opposite of isolation. The danger of sectarianism is promptly overcome in Chiara's universal embrace of humanity. Her emphasis on loving one's neighbor and on the "art of loving" that comes from the gospel made her, and with her everyone who follows the Focolare spirituality, open to every person they encounter. She wrote:

> The first characteristic of Christian love is that it reaches out "*to all.*" This way of loving requires that we love everyone, as God does, without distinction. We do not choose between who is nice or unpleasant, old or young, countryman or foreigner, black, white or yellow, European or American, African or Asian, Christian or Jew, Muslim or Hindu.… In today's terminology we could say that this kind of love avoids every form of discrimination.[38]

There is, however, a distinction between those who are the object of one's love and those who are included in Chiara's concept of unity. Although her definition of unity is clear, her writings are sometimes contradictory when describing to whom this unity refers. Is Chiara

---

38. Chiara Lubich, *The Art of Loving* (Hyde Park, NY: New City Press, 2010), 21.

speaking about unity among those who follow this collective way of sanctity? Among Catholics who are united by the bond of the Eucharist, as the statutes of the Movement read?[39] Among Christians of different Churches who believe Jesus' message? Among people of different religions or people of good will?

An in-depth study of Chiara's understanding of unity would go beyond the scope of this book. It is sufficient to mention for now that there was undoubtedly an evolution in Chiara's understanding of unity with the passing of time. During the first years of her spirituality, Chiara interpreted the "all" of John 17:21 as embracing the whole human family: "As Christians we must be committed to the *ut omnes*[40] and then, first of all, we must renew our conviction that everyone is called to unity, because God loves everyone."[41]

39. "Through the Eucharist and reciprocal love, they will have the conditions necessary to obtain the gift of unity asked by Jesus in his priestly prayer to the Father: 'May they all be one, as you, Father, are in me and I in you, that they also may be in us' (Jn 17:21)." Work of Mary (Focolare Movement), *General Statutes.* translated from the Italian *Opera di Maria—Statuti Generali* (New York: Focolare Movement, 2008), 13.
40. This is Lubich's usual way of referring to Jn 17:21, abbreviating the Latin *ut omnes unum sint* "May they all be one." See Lubich, *Essential Writings*, 19, footnote.
41. Lubich, *Art of Loving*, 26.

As time went by, however, and as she studied John's Gospel more and more, she emphasized that the unity that Christ talks about refers to the Christian community. Her concept of unity is therefore linked to ecumenism:

> The only genuine Christian reconciler will be the one who knows how to love others with the very charity of God, which brings Christ to light in each person, which goes out to all (Jesus died for the whole human race), which always takes the initiative... And the Churches too should love with this love. "That the love with which you have loved me may be in them, and I in them" (Jn 17:26), Jesus prayed. And we instead are always ready to forget his testament, to scandalize the world with our divisions, a world we should be winning for him.[42]

Ecumenism, therefore, if lived according to John's Gospel, will be a witness for those who do not believe in Jesus.

As demonstrated in the above quote, Chiara, very much in the Johannine spirit, linked the concept of unity of the elect to the idea of "mission" to the whole world. For Chiara, the particularism of unity among Christ's followers

---

42. Lubich, *Essential Writings*, 328.

needs to go hand in hand with the universalism of a vocation of all humankind to unity. She explained this to a group of young people in 1989:

> Jesus prayed: 'Father, may all be one' (Jn 17:21). His prayer was for the unity of Christians, of course, but it has repercussions on the entire world, because unity among Christians is the premise, guarantee and foretaste of unity in the entire world.[43]

Unity among people who live the same spirituality is, therefore, a "launching pad" for bringing Christ's love to all humanity. Unity, for Chiara, is God's call for humankind and the deepest aspiration of every person.

This concept, although more clearly defined towards the end of her life, was already present in Chiara's early writings. A letter to a group of Franciscans in Assisi explicitly mentioned John 17:19, linking "sanctity" and "unity" with the universalism of a Christian call:

> Jesus said...'And for their sakes I sanctify myself, so that they also may be sanctified in truth' (Jn 17:19). To

---

43. Chiara Lubich, "Jesus is the Way" (Address to Italian Youth during World Youth Day at Santiago de Compostela, Spain: August 16, 1989).

accomplish the Unity of all Assisi and the world, stay united with each other. It's the only way.[44]

Sanctity and Individual Salvation: Lubich's Eschatology in the Light of John 17:11b-19

A writing of Chiara's from the 1950s summarizes her eschatological view. She began by saying that "an individualistic life… stands in contradiction to the Christian life." She continued by insisting:

> Love generates communion: communion as the basis of the Christian life and as its summit. In this communion a person no longer goes to God alone, but travels in company.[45]

This later text elaborates on that concept:

> The Lord doesn't ask us for an individual holiness, but for a communitarian holiness in which each of us must help our neighbor to become a saint. Then our neighbor will do likewise with his or her neighbor, as in a chain reaction. This is the kind of sanctity which could be verified and highlighted someday for

44. Lubich, *Early Letters*, 98.
45. Lubich, *Essential Writings*, 100.

the edification of many in the Church:
a collective sanctity.[46]

The question that comes up when looking at these texts is the following: Is Chiara's "collective sanctity" or traveling to God "in company" very different from John's view?

In order to answer the above question, we need to briefly analyze John's eschatology. In most of John's Gospel, one can find that the eternal life that Christ promises is already in the possession of those who accept his message. This is what most exegetes call "realized eschatology." For John, the faith in Jesus, light of the world, in the present is the judgment that separates those who believe from those who come under condemnation.

Realized eschatology is, for scholars like Moule, the main proof that John's Gospel is individualistic. In his study of individualism in the fourth gospel, Moule affirms that John's Gospel is:

> ...the gospel, par excellence, of the approach of the single soul to God: this is the part of Scripture to which one turns first when trying to direct an

---

46. Lubich, "Holiness of the Masses," 23.

enquirer to his own, personal appropria-
tion of salvation.[47]

Moule does not agree with what he feels is a
contemporary trend that looks at John's Gospel
as "corporate." True, he concedes, community in
John is important to an extent, but any idea of an
eschatology which is already fulfilled on earth
refers to each person's acceptance of the salvation that Jesus offers. Therefore, it is "inherently
bound to show an individualistic tendency: the
more fully realized, the narrower the scope."[48]

John's future or apocalyptic eschatology comes
up in very few texts of his gospel. Moule sees a
sharp contrast between an individual realized
eschatology and a corporate eschatology at the
end of times. According to Moule's study, the
future eschatology—which is present in John's
epistles much more than in the gospel—may be
intended as a correction of an excessive individualistic reading of the gospel.[49]

A later study by John O'Grady explains the
main reason for John's individualism in the fact
that the fourth gospel "emphasizes the need for

---

47. C.D.F. Moule, "The Individualism of the Fourth Gospel," *Novum Testamentum* 5 (1962), in *The Composition of John's Gospel: Selected Studies from Novum
Testamentum*, ed. David E. Orton (Boston: Brill
Academic Pub, 1999), 35.
48. Ibid., 23.
49. Ibid., 32.

the individual believer to respond in faith to the final revealer, mediator and envoy of God. This is the central thought and always most necessary for the understanding of the gospel."[50] These studies confirm Käsemann's view of the evangelist as an "anti-ecclesiastical, pietistic believer."[51]

These statements may be a misinterpretation of what is intended by the concept of "communitarian" or "corporate" when talking about salvation. They seem to look at it as a kind of Christianity where individual responsibility is at least blurred if not totally annihilated. Instead, John's emphasis on the individual acceptance of Jesus does not exclude a communitarian perspective. Actually, it is precisely each individual's conscious act of faith in Jesus that forms the basis for a true community, where persons who have made that choice gather in unity. There are multiple images in John's Gospel that accentuate this concept of collectivity, such as the vineyard in chapter 15 or the flock in chapter 10.[52] Similarly, Rossé points out that, in John's Gospel, "faith, being a

---

50. John F. O'Grady, "Individualism and Johannine Ecclesiology," *Biblical Theology Bulletin: A Journal of Bible and Theology* 1975 5:227, http://btb.sagepub.com/content/5/3/227.citation [accessed June 17, 2013], 260–61.

51. Ernst Käsemann, "Ketzer und Zeuge," in *Exegetische Versuche und Besinnungen* (1960), 168 ff., quoted in Moule, "Individualism," 34–35.

52. Thus, Brown, *Introduction*, 227.

personal encounter with Christ, does not enclose the believer in a private and solitary devotion to him; on the contrary, it even structures him in depth as a person open to others." [53]

Chiara emphasized an analogous concept:

> The Focolarini are asked to live a life similar to Mary's. It is a life both individual and collective, where the plurality of persons who live a life of holiness together increases the holiness of each person, and the holiness of each enriches that of the others. [54]

Unity becomes the sign par excellence of Christian life. Therefore, the communion of humanity is not reserved for the final judgment, but in accordance with the "realized eschatology" present in John's Gospel, it already takes place where Christians live true unity. Chiara said:

> Whoever lives unity, lives Jesus, and lives in the Father. He or she lives in heaven, in paradise always: the earthly here, made paradise through the hundredfold, and the heavenly on high, through life eternal. [55]

---

53. Rossé, *Spirituality of Communion,* 57.
54. Lubich, *Essential Writings,* 50.
55. Ibid., 109.

An indication of this realized eschatology is the "full joy" that Jesus promises his disciples. Bultmann affirms that the fullness of joy or χαρὰ, in Judaism and other ancient cultures, describes future salvation.[56] John 16:20 has also a clear accent on future joy ("You will suffer, but your suffering will turn into joy.") Yet in 17:13 ("Now I am coming to you, and I speak these things in the world, so that they may have my joy made full in them"), it means joy already in the present without losing the idea of eschatological joy.

Chiara expressed this concept in her letter to a group of Franciscans in Assisi:

> That Unity in which Love dwells will give you strength to face every external disunity and to fill every void. Do this as your sacrosanct duty, even though it brings you immense joy! Jesus promised the fullness of joy to those who live Unity![57]

---

56. Bultmann, *Gospel of John*, 507.
57. Lubich, *Early Letters*, 98.

Conclusion

Communitarian sanctity is not a new concept; it goes back to the beginning of the history of salvation. As Deuteronomy reminds us, the wonderful history of God's chosen people began with a collective experience of sanctity, a holiness shared by the people of Israel as a communal identity:[1]

> For you are a people holy to the Lord your God; the Lord your God has chosen you out of all the peoples on earth to be his people, his treasured possession.
>
> Dt 7:6

Chiara Lubich offers a spiritual way that, although daring and innovative, has solid roots in Church tradition. She applies John 17 to speak to today's Christians of the need to establish deep bonds of unity, based on the oneness and distinction that exists among the Persons of the Most Holy Trinity. Her desire for a collective sanctity is an invitation for contemporary

---

1. Tiziana Longhitano, "Journeying Together Towards Holiness Is Possible," *Charisms in Unity* 20, no. 3 (2012): 8.

Christians to not conform to a personal ascetic way, but to be a collective witness of Christ's love to the world, as John was exhorting the communities of the first disciples of Jesus.

Mutual love—a love that attracts God's divine gift of unity—is, therefore, Chiara's point of departure. Somehow it allows Christians to live the fullness of God's life already on this earth and prepare for eternal life.

Christians cannot, however, be restricted to a comfortable group closed in upon itself. That would not be what God desires. Chiara encourages believers in Christ to have a universal scope—the thrust to bring Christ's love, first of all through the witness of their love, to all humanity.

This text of 1999, a kind of spiritual testament, summarizes these thoughts. It expresses Chiara's dream for the Movement she founded:

> I remember the words I read with my first companions, perhaps as long ago as 1944, on the feast of Christ the King: "Ask of me, and I will make the nations your heritage, and the ends of the earth your possession" (Ps 2:8). On that day, we asked for it with faith. The Movement has truly reached the very ends of the earth. And in this *new people* are *represented* the peoples of all the earth.

Their number is such that the wish of my bishop in 1956…: "Would that there were a legion of Focolarini!" has now come true. He, who had hoped that standing by the Focolarini would help him to heaven, will be seeing this from above.

What, just now, would be my last wish? I wish that the Work of Mary, at the end of the ages, when it will be waiting, united, to appear before Jesus forsaken and risen, may be able to repeat to him, making its own the words of the Belgian theologian Jacques Leclercq, words I always find moving: "On your day, my God, I shall come to you.… I shall come to you, my God … with my wildest dream: to bring you the world in my arms."

"Father, may they all be one!"[2]

---

2. Lubich, *Essential Writings*, 369.

Bibliography

Abignente, Lucia. "Journeying Towards Holiness Together: Chiara Lubich's Witness." *Charisms in Unity* 20, no. 3 (2012): 14–20.

Aland, B., Aland, K. and Newman, B., eds. *Nestle-Aland Novum Testamentum Graece with Concise English-Greek Dictionary*. 27 ed. Louisville, KY: American Bible Society, 2005.

Attridge, Harold W. "How Priestly Is the 'High Priestly Prayer' of John 17?" *Catholic Biblical Quarterly* 75, no. 1: 1–14. *ATLA Religion Database with ATLASerials*, EBSCOhost (accessed January 6, 2014).

Barrett, C.K. *The Gospel According to St. John: An Introduction with Commentary and Notes on the Greek Text*. London: SPCK Publishing, 1988.

Brodie, Thomas L. *The Gospel According to John: A Literary and Theological Commentary*. New York: Oxford University Press, USA, 1997.

Brown, Raymond E. *An Introduction to the Gospel of John*. Edited, updated, introduced and concluded by Francis J. Moloney. New York: Anchor Bible, 2003.

_____. *The Community of the Beloved Disciple.* New York: Paulist Press, 1979.

_____. "The Gospel According to John XIII-XXI." *Anchor Bible Series.* Vol. 29A. Garden City: Anchor Bible, 1966.

Bultmann, Rudolf. *The Gospel of John: a Commentary.* Philadelphia: Westminster John Knox Press, 1971.

Carson, D.A. *The Farewell Discourse and Final Prayer of Jesus: an Exposition of John 14–17.* Grand Rapids, Mich.: Baker Book House, 1980.

Ciardi, Fabio. "What Kind of Holiness Comes from the Spirituality of Communion?" *Charisms in Unity* 20, no. 3 (2012): 6–13.

Dodd, C.H. *The Interpretation of the Fourth Gospel.* 1953. Reprint, London: The Syndics of the Cambridge University Press, 1955.

Elowsky, Joel C., ed. *John 11–21.* Vol. 4b of *Ancient Christian Commentary on Scripture.* Downers Grove, IL: InterVarsity Press, 2007.

Käsemann, Ernst. *The Testament of Jesus: A Study of the Gospel of John in the Light of Chapter 17.* Philadelphia: Fortress Press, 1968.

Leahy, Brendan. *Ecclesial Movements and Communities: Origins, Significance and Issues.* Hyde Park, NY: New City Press, 2011.

Longhitano, Tiziana. "Journeying Together Towards Holiness Is Possible." *Charisms in Unity* 20, no. 3 (2012): 3–5.

Lubich, Chiara. *A New Way: the Spirituality of Unity.* Hyde Park, NY: New City Press, 2006.

_____. *Early Letters: at the Origins of a New Spirituality.* Hyde Park, NY: New City Press, 2012.

_____. *Essential Writings.* Edited by Michel Vandeleene. Hyde Park, NY: New City Press, 2007.

_____. "Holiness of the Masses." *Charisms in Unity* 20, no. 3 (2012): 21–24.

_____. *Jesus—the Heart of His Message: Unity and Jesus Forsaken.* 2nd ed. Hyde Park, NY: New City Press, 1997.

_____. *Journey: Spiritual Insights.* New York: New City Press, 1984.

_____. *Journey to Heaven: Spiritual Thoughts to Live.* Hyde Park, NY: New City Press, 1997.

_____. *On the Holy Journey.* New York: New City Press, 1988.

_____. *Santi Insieme.* Rome: Città Nuova Editrice, 1994.

_____. *The Art of Loving.* Hyde Park, NY: New City Press, 2010.

Masters, Thomas, and Amy Uelmen. *Focolare: Living a Spirituality of Unity in the United States.* Hyde Park, NY: New City Press, 2011.

Moule, C.D.F. "The Individualism of the Fourth Gospel." *Novum Testamentum* 5 (1962), 21–40. In *The Composition of John's Gospel: Selected Studies from Novum Testamentum*, edited by David E. Orton. Boston: Brill Academic Pub, 1999.

Norris, Thomas J. *The Trinity—Life of God, Hope for Humanity: Towards a Theology of Communion.* Hyde Park, NY: New City Press, 2009.

O'Day, Gail R. "The Gospel of John: Introduction, Commentary, and Reflections." *The New Interpreter's Bible: A Commentary in Twelve Volumes.* Vol. 9. Nashville, Tennessee: Abingdon Press, 2001.

O'Grady, John F. "Individual and Community in John." Ph.D. diss., Pontifical Biblical Institute. Rome: 1978.

_____. "Individualism and Johannine Ecclesiology." *Biblical Theology Bulletin: A Journal of Bible and Theology* 1975 5:227. http://btb.sagepub.com/content/5/3/227.citation [accessed June 17, 2013].

Pinckaers, Servais. *The Sources of Christian Ethics.* Washington, D.C.: Catholic University of America Press, 1995.

Potterie, Ignace de la. *La Vérité dans Saint Jean.* 2 vols. Analecta Biblica. Rome: Biblical Institute Press, 1977.

Ratzinger, Joseph (Pope Benedict XVI). *Jesus of Nazareth.* New York: Doubleday, 2007.

_____. *Jesus of Nazareth. Part Two: Holy Week—from the Entrance into Jerusalem to the Resurrection.* San Francisco: Ignatius Press, 2011.

_____. "The Transmission of Divine Revelation." In *Commentary on the Documents of Vatican II*, edited by Herbert Vorgrimler, vol 3, 155–198. New York: Herder and Herder, 1969.

Rossé, Gérard. *The Spirituality of Communion: a New Approach to the Johannine Writings.* Hyde Park, NY: New City Press, 1998.

Schnackenburg, Rudolf. *The Gospel According to St. John: Volume 3.* New York: Crossroad/Herder & Herder, 1983.

Tecilla, Marco. "Santificarsi Insieme: Alcuni Strumenti." *Gen's* 34, no. 3/4 (2004): 68–73.

Work of Mary (Focolare Movement). *General Statutes.* Translated from the Italian *Opera di Maria—Statuti Generali.* Provisional Translation. New York: Focolare Movement, 2008.

NCP

NEW CITY PRESS
of the Focolare
Hyde Park, New York

New City Press is one of more than 20 publishing houses sponsored by the Focolare, a movement founded by Chiara Lubich to help bring about the realization of Jesus' prayer: "That all may be one" (John 17:21). In view of that goal, New City Press publishes books and resources that enrich the lives of people and help all to strive toward the unity of the entire human family. We are a member of the Association of Catholic Publishers.

Further Reading

5 Steps to Facing Suffering Geraldine Guadagno			
	paperback	978-1-56548-502-0	$4.95
	ebook	978-1-56548-570-9	$3.95
The Cry of Jesus Crucified and Forsaken Chiara Lubich			
		978-1-56548-159-6	$11.95
Early Letters Chiara Lubich		978-1-56548-432-0	$15.95
Essential Writings: Spirituality, Dialogue, Culture Chiara Lubich			
	paperback	978-1-56548-259-3	$24.95
	ebook	978-1-56548-347-7	$9.95
Introduction to the Abba School Abba School	978-1-56548-176-3		$11.95
The Choice of Jesus Forsaken Chiara Lubich	978-1-56548-506-8		$13.95
Unity Chiara Lubich		978-1-56548-593-8	$14.95

Periodicals
Living City Magazine,
www.livingcitymagazine.com

www.ingramcontent.com/pod-product-compliance
Lightning Source LLC
Chambersburg PA
CBHW060709030426
42337CB00017B/2821